Date Due

BRODART, INC   Cat. No. 23 233   Printed in U.S.A

LOGGERS AND
RAILROAD WORKERS

SETTLING THE WEST

LOGGERS AND RAILROAD WORKERS

MIMI WINSLOW

TWENTY–FIRST CENTURY BOOKS

A Division of Henry Holt and Company

Twenty-First Century Books
A Division of Henry Holt and Company, Inc.
115 West 18th Street
New York, NY 10011

Henry Holt ® and colophon are trademarks of
Henry Holt and Company, Inc.
Publishers since 1866

Library of Congress Cataloging–in–Publication Data
Winslow, Mimi.
Loggers and railroad workers / Mimi Winslow.
p. cm. — (Settling the West)
Includes bibliographical references and index.
Summary: Describes the lives of people involved in logging and the expansion of the
railroads in the American West during the second half of the nineteenth century.
1. Loggers—West (U.S.)—History—19th century—Juvenile literature. 2. Logging—
West (U.S.)—History—19th century—Juvenile literature. 3. Railroads—United
States—Employees—History—19th century—Juvenile literature. 4. Railroads—United
States—History—19th century—Juvenile literature. [1. Logging—West (U.S)—History.
2. Railroads—West (U.S.)—History. 3. West (U.S.) History.] I. Title. II. Series.
HD8039.L92U59 1995
338.7′63498′0978—dc20   94–39903
                                                                       CIP
                                                                       AC

ISBN 0–8050–2997–4
First Edition 1995

Cover design by Kelly Soong
Interior design by Helene Berinsky

Printed in the United States of America
All first editions are printed on acid-free paper ∞.
10 9 8 7 6 5 4 3 2 1

Photo Credits
pp. 2, 16, 17, 30, 48, 49, 63, 68, 74, 83: North Wind Picture Archives; pp. 19, 52:
Montana Historical Society, Helena; pp. 24, 38, 51, 59, 61, 71, 77, 81: Museum of
History and Industry; p. 26 (all): Potlatch Corp.; pp. 35, 37, 43, 54: California State
Railroad Museum; p. 40: Oregon Historical Society/OrHi 61616; p. 65: Pemco Webster
& Stevens Collection/Museum of History and Industry; p. 78: Idaho State Historical
Society/64-26.26.

EDITOR'S NOTE

A great deal of research went into finding interesting first-person accounts that would give the reader a vivid picture of life on the western frontier. In order to retain the "flavor" of these accounts, original spelling and punctuation have been kept in most instances.

History told in the words of men and women who lived at the time lets us become a part of their lives . . . lives of ordinary people who met extraordinary challenges to settle the West.

—P.C.

**This book is dedicated to
Chris, Megan, and Nick Tompkins.**

ACKNOWLEDGMENTS

I gratefully acknowledge the encouragement and guidance of Judith Bentley, field editor of the series. I truly appreciate the assistance of my husband, Christopher Tompkins, who solved many of the computer problems encountered during this adventure and encouraged my efforts. Finally, I am grateful for the forbearance of my children, Megan and Nick, while I was preoccupied with researching and writing, and for their encouragement.

—*M.W.*

CONTENTS

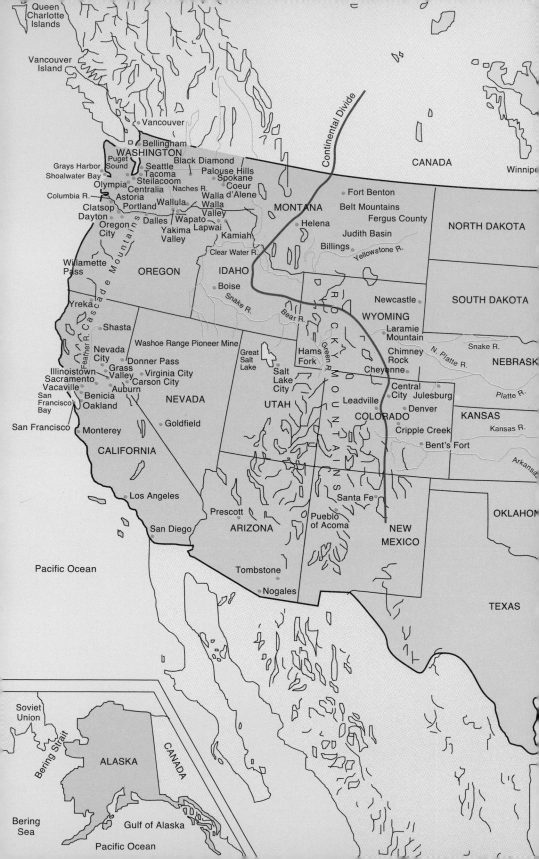

Queen
Charlotte
Islands

Vancouver
Island

Vancouver

Bellingham

WASHINGTON

Puget
Sound
Grays Harbor
Shoalwater Bay
Seattle
Tacoma
Steilacoom
Olympia
Centralia
Columbia R.
Astoria
Clatsop
Portland
Dayton
Oregon
City
Dalles

Black Diamond
Palouse Hills
Spokane
Coeur
d'Alene
Naches R.
Walla d'Alene
Wallula
Walla
Walla
Valley
Wapato
Lapwai
Yakima
Valley
Kamiah
Clear Water R.

CANADA

Continental Divide

Fort Benton

Belt Mountains

MONTANA
Fergus County

Helena

Judith Basin

Billings

Yellowstone R.

NORTH DAKOTA

Willamette
Pass

OREGON

Cascade Mountains

IDAHO

Boise

Snake R.

Bear R.

SOUTH DAKOTA

Newcastle

WYOMING

Yreka

Shasta

Washoe Range Pioneer Mine

Feather R.

Nevada
City
Donner Pass
Grass
Valley
Illinoistown
Sacramento
Vacaville
Benicia
Virginia City
Carson City
Auburn
San
Francisco
Bay
Oakland

NEVADA

Goldfield

Great
Salt
Lake

Salt
Lake
City

UTAH

Laramie
Mountain

ROCKY MOUNTAINS

Hams
Fork

Green R.

Chimney
Rock
Cheyenne

Leadville

N. Platte R.

Snake R.

NEBRASKA

Platte R.

Central
City Julesburg

Denver

KANSAS

Colorado

San Francisco
Monterey

CALIFORNIA

Los Angeles

Cripple Creek

Bent's Fort

Kansas R.

Arkansas

San Diego

Prescott

ARIZONA

Pueblo
of Acoma

Santa Fe

OKLAHOMA

Tombstone

Nogales

NEW
MEXICO

Pacific Ocean

TEXAS

Soviet
Union

Bering Strait

ALASKA

CANADA

Bering
Sea

Gulf of Alaska

Pacific Ocean

SETTLING THE WEST
Many of the places mentioned in
the series are located on this map.

MAINE

VT

NH

Lowell

NEW YORK

Boston

MA

Taunton

Seneca Falls

CT

RI

NNESOTA

MICHIGAN

WISCONSIN

Plainfield

New York City

PENNSYLVANIA

IOWA

Dubuque

Philadelphia

NJ

ouncil Bluffs

Baltimore

maha

OHIO

MARYLAND

Nauvoo

WASHINGTON

St. Joseph

INDIANA

ILLINOIS

Missouri R.

St. Louis

WEST
VIRGINIA

Independence

VIRGINIA

MISSOURI

KENTUCKY

ARKANSAS

NORTH
CAROLINA

TENNESSEE

SOUTH
CAROLINA

ed R.

GEORGIA

Atlantic Ocean

MISSISSIPPI

ALABAMA

LOUISIANA

FLORIDA

Gulf of Mexico

CUBA

MAJOR TRAILS TO THE WEST

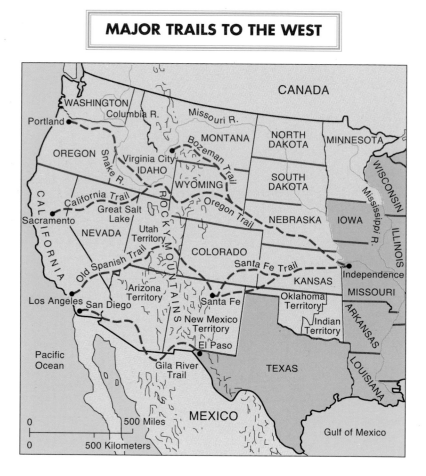

INTRODUCTION

Imagine it is January 1, 1840. The United States officially became a country only fifty-some years ago, when the Constitution was ratified on June 21, 1788. All twenty-six states are east of the Missouri River. The continent west of the river is known and used mainly by Native American peoples and trappers.

Now imagine it is January 1, 1920. The forty-eight states stretch from the Atlantic Ocean to the Pacific. Cities, industries, productive farms, and sprawling ranches exist where there was wilderness only eighty years earlier.

What happened to make these dramatic changes possible?

Two groups of people helped make it easier for others to settle the West permanently: railroad workers and loggers. Without railroads and wood, developing and populating the West would have been slower and more difficult for the settlers. This book tells the story of how pioneers in railroading and logging helped build the West. In many cases you will read about their lives in their own words, or from newspaper reports written at the time. You will also learn how much their lives and their work changed in a short time.

1

WESTERN LOGGING FROM SETTLEMENT TO STEAM

Along the Pacific Coast the land was heavily forested, as a song from the nineteenth century tells us:

> Arriving flat broke in mid-winter
> I found it enveloped in fog
> And covered all over with timber
> As thick as the hair on a dog. . . .
>
> As I looked at the prospect so gloomy
> The tears trickled over my face;
> For I felt that my travels had brought me
> To the edge of the jumping-off place. . . .
>
> I took up a claim in the forest,
> And set myself down hard to toil.
> For two years I chopped and I labored,
> But I never got down to the soil. . . .
>
> —"The Old Settler"[1]

People had cut down the trees in the western United States long before there was westward migration and long before there was a United States. For hundreds of years Northwest coastal Indian peoples had felled giant red cedars, using stone hatchets, sharpened mussel shells, and controlled fire at the tree base. The Nootka people cut two deep wedges in the living cedar tree, one above the other, as far apart as the desired length of a canoe, and let storm winds snap the tree apart at the right places. Native peoples built large houses and fashioned totem poles for family and community use. They also made clothing, bedding, mats, and baskets from the bark. But unlike later loggers, they did not sell the wood. They cut down only the trees they needed for immediate purposes, and they wasted nothing.

When the English built Fort Vancouver alongside the Columbia River and later imported a water-powered sawmill from London in 1827, commercial logging—logging trees to sell the timber—began in the West. The Hudson's Bay Company exported northwest cedar and Douglas fir to Hawaii and other distant places. A small lumber industry also existed in California, which was at that time a province of Mexico.

Soon after 1840 a small number of Americans and European immigrants began to move to the Oregon Territory and to California. The story of rapid settlement of the American West really begins with the discovery of gold in California—and the discovery of gold resulted from a man's need for board lumber. In 1839 John Sutter, a Swiss citizen, emigrated to Mexican California and was granted 50,000 acres in the Sacramento Valley. There he built a fort and a trading post selling fresh supplies to immigrants coming from Missouri to homestead. The settlers, whose provisions were exhausted by the long journey across the country, wanted to buy flour and other supplies.

"I was very much in need of a sawmill to get lumber to finish my flouring-mill . . . likewise, for other buildings, fences, etc. for the small village of Yerba Buena, now San Francisco,"[2] recalled Sutter. So in 1847 he entered into a partnership with John Marshall to build a sawmill on his property along the river and to raft the sawed boards to Sutter's fort.

On January 24, 1848, Marshall found gold in the mill-race. The California Gold Rush began as soon as news of the discovery reached the East Coast. "What a great misfortune was this sudden gold discovery to me!" wrote Sutter. "It has just broken up and ruined my hard, industrious and restless laborers. . . . From my mill buildings I reaped no benefit whatever; the mill-stones, even, have been stolen from me . . . all was abandoned at an immense loss."[3]

The trickle of pioneers in the early 1840s into both California and the Oregon Territory became a flood after gold was discovered. Before they could make any use of the land, the newcomers had to clear the trees. Many of the immigrants were novices at cutting them down, and the results could be deadly, as the letters of Louise Clappe, an early California immigrant, reveal. She wrote her sister: "I received an immense fright the other morning. I was sitting by the fire, quietly reading . . . when a mighty crash against the side of the cabin, shaking it to the foundation, threw me suddenly upon my knees . . . a large tree which was felled this morning . . . rolled down from the brow of the hill . . . and its having struck a rock a few feet from the house, losing thereby the most of its force, had alone saved us from

The first settlers used axes and saws to clear the land.

utter destruction. . . . Every one who saw the forest giant descending the hill with the force of a mighty torrent, expected to see the cabin instantly prostrated to the earth."[4] These mishaps occurred frequently, whether in clearing the land for a cabin site or in cutting trees for sale. Those doing the cutting were as much at risk as anyone in the path.

Some pioneers were able to profit from the tree-clearing activity that had to be done in any event by selling the logs or running sawmills themselves. Marianne Hunsaker's family left Illinois for the Oregon Territory in 1846, when she was four years old. She recalled that in 1847, "father built a sawmill on the Columbia [River] near St.

Helens. . . . In the fall of 1848 Captain Crosby bought all the lumber Father had, to take to San Francisco, for it was believed the discovery of gold at Sutter's Mill would cause a building boom at San Francisco."[5] The California gold had made its way north; Marianne's father was paid for his lumber in gold dust.

Many shippers tried to satisfy the voracious demand for lumber. Mining required strong timbers to support the tunnels and board lumber for sluices and troughs. Lumber also was needed to build homes and businesses in rapidly growing mining and trading towns. To meet the demand, two things happened. Some men cut trees, and others soon brought in sawmills powered by steam engines.

Within weeks of their arrival, even before they had

Often, strong timbers were needed to keep the surrounding boulders from falling and sealing the entrance to a mine.

staked out a homestead to claim on Puget Sound, the first pioneer settlers in Seattle were visited by a ship from California seeking to buy a cargo of log piles. Arthur Denny, a member of that pioneer group, remembered: "We had no team [of animals] at the time, but some of us went to work cutting the timber nearest the water, and rolled and hauled in by hand. . . . Our first year on our claims (1852) was spent in building homes and getting out piles and timber as a means of support."[6] When the Denny party chose their homesteads, they claimed land along Puget Sound with the deepest harbor and with abundant trees. Harbors had to be deep enough for log schooners to load the wood without getting stuck. The lumber ships to which they delivered the timber also brought in most of their supplies. There were no wagon roads, and the nearest places to buy supplies or sell anything were many miles away.

Other early Pacific settlers turned to running mills that sawed the trees into boards or timbers suitable for bridges, wharf supports, shingles, or building lumber. Cutting a log into usable lumber can be done by hand: a wedge can be hammered into the wood and hit forcefully to split it, and one or two men, depending on the size of the log, can saw the timber into boards. Captain John Burns wrote about building a fifty-ton ship in 1853: "There being as yet no sawmill except Mike Summers' at Olympia . . . James Keymes and myself sawed, by hand, every foot of the lumber used in her construction (makes my back ache yet thinking of it.)"[7]

Businessmen quickly recognized the opportunity the gold rush and migration presented. Henry Yesler moved from Portland, Oregon, to the Seattle area only one year after it was settled in 1851. He was looking for a heavily forested location for his steam sawmill. Within ten years he had built a business employing twenty mill workers. Most of his lumber was shipped to San Francisco, but some was used to build Seattle. Arthur Denny wrote in his memoirs that his first home was a log cabin, but that as soon as Yesler "began to cut lumber we built frame houses and vacated our log cabins as speedily as possible."[8]

Even in the pioneer days in the West, in addition to small companies like Yesler's and homesteaders like the Hunsakers, who ran a mill on the side, there were large lumber companies. When Caroline Leighton toured the Pacific Coast in the 1860s, she kept a travel journal record-

An early sawmill like this one might be run by just a few men, but in some areas huge sawmills employed hundreds of men.

ing her experiences. About the large mills she wrote that it seemed "as if we might perhaps be living in feudal time, these great mill-owners have such authority in the settlements. Some of them possess very large tracts of land, have hundreds of men in their employ, own steamboats and hotels, and have large stores of general merchandise, in connection with their mill-business."[9]

The Pope & Talbot Company was such a company. It began by buying Henry Yesler's lumber and carrying it to San Francisco on its log schooner. The next year the company built a steam sawmill; within four years it was cutting enough timber to fill a log vessel every week. By 1862 it owned almost 35,000 acres and had the right to cut the trees from thousands more acres owned by homesteaders. The large mills had a diverse workforce, employing South Americans, Hawaiians, European immigrants, and both black and white American citizens.

"They sometimes provide amusements for the men . . . to keep them from resorting to drink," continued Ms. Leighton, "and encourage them to send for their families, and to make gardens around their homes."[10] Pope & Talbot provided unmarried mill hands and loggers with a 400-person bunkhouse and married employees with separate homes, and housed its Indian workers across the bay from the white employees. These conditions in the Pope & Talbot mills were not typical, however; smaller mills were much less generous.

The pioneer days of western logging also included many people who were only temporarily loggers. William Vaughan tried many different ways to make a living after crossing the country by wagon train and arriving in the Oregon Territory in 1851. He first prospected for gold in

Canada. When that was unsuccessful, he wrote, he "set sail and landed at Olympia June 15, 1852. Olympia was then a settlement consisting of a few log cabins. . . . I now went to work on the Sound getting out piles and square timber. At this time there were only two ox teams on the Sound. In the spring of '53 I got a team of four yoke of oxen and went to work loading vessels for myself, employing six men and getting $40 per day over expenses."[11]

Oxen were important in western logging because of their strength. Western trees weighed too much for men to move alone, unless they could roll the timber downhill. Without oxen to drag the fallen trees, a man could not move them in logs long enough to be used by sawmills. A few years later these teams of animals would be replaced by a steam-powered engine, but until it was invented, a team of horses or oxen was a necessity.

"When there were no vessels [wanting to buy timber] I logged for the Chambers mill, making about $20 a day. This was the first mill on the Sound on tide water."[12] Vaughan continued to go from job to job, returning to logging several times. He followed new opportunities because none of his business attempts created the degree of success and wealth he wanted.

What was involved in being a pioneer logger? Axes were big, heavy, and required strength to swing repeatedly through the bark and wood of a large tree. Attie Long, the daughter of a Colorado pioneer who had lost his health in the Civil War, had vivid recollections of her father's daily routine. "Pa was so well by this time that he could take a heavy double-bitted ax and help chop down large trees and log them to the saw mill in Florissant,"[13] she wrote.

"He bought a pair of oxen for this purpose and this

was his means of making a living. The logs were cut on the hill and had to be dragged down to a level place before they could be loaded on a wagon. Pa would put a heavy iron log chain around one end of the log, to which he would hitch one of the oxen and in this fashion drag it down the hill."[14]

"A narrow path had to be cleared before this could be done,"[15] Attie continued. All loggers faced the problem of obstacles between the fallen tree and the destination; they meant more time and labor and less income. These obstacles could be anything—other trees or stumps, or soft ground in which the logs or the wagons that carried them could get stuck.

"When sufficient logs had been brought down, Pa helped put them on the log wagon which was a rather low contraption with small wheels and broad iron tires to keep it from sinking into the soft ground. The wagon would not hold more than three large logs. The same iron chain that had been used to drag them down the mountain was used to bind the logs onto the wagon. Sometimes this chain would break and the logs would roll off with a terrific thud. Then, maybe the wagon would upset and things such as this were surely enough to make a preacher swear. . . ."[16] Logs rolling off wagons were frequently more than just a frustration, however; there are many reports of men being crushed to death by falling logs.

Mr. Long was a homesteading logger who worked for himself and by himself and did everything himself. By contrast, in the larger Pacific Northwest logging companies, men were employed to do specialized jobs. There were choppers who actually brought the trees down. The ax was commonly used until it was replaced by the crosscut saw.

The two-man saw was the only tool that could be used on the enormous California redwoods and northwestern Douglas firs; no ax could cut through them.

The men who cut the downed trees into logs small enough to be dragged by oxen or horses were known as "buckers." A single Douglas fir could provide four logs, each 24 or 32 feet long and 10 feet in diameter, weighing up to 100 tons. On hilly ground the bucker might stand on the slope below the fallen tree so that gravity would help pull the saw through the wood, but when the log segment was cut free, it could roll over him and kill him.

Often six to eight oxen were needed to "yard," or drag, one of these huge trees to where it would be loaded with other trees. One of the earliest yarding methods was to hitch oxen to enormous two-wheeled carts. George Hunsby, a second-generation logger whose family worked in the timber business for many years, described the carts: "The wheels themselves was about eight, nine feet tall. And an enormous axle that run across between the wheels and then they would hoist the end of the log up against the axle so it was free of the ground . . . that would reduce the friction. . . ."[17]

To make it even easier for the animals, "skid roads" were introduced. Skid roads were paths made of felled trees that had been stripped of limbs and bark to make them smooth, for the less friction there was, the easier it was for the animals to pull the load. The paths were called skid roads because the trees skidded their way down to their destination.

Ten or more animals frequently worked together to pull a load of logs over the skid road. Large logging companies had four to six dozen bulls working all day.

"Bullwhackers" were the men in charge of them. The bull-whacker was one of the best-paid workers. The oxen he commanded were valuable, and he trained, fed, and cared for them. He kept them under control solely by verbal commands, a whip, and a pointed stick called a goad.

The bullwhacker was often assisted by a young teenager whose job was to lubricate the skids. He spread whatever slippery substance was available to help the logs slide with less friction. Fish oil, bear grease, sheep fat, spoiled butter—all were used. It was the smelliest job in the industry! It required both a strong nose and a strong back.

Ted Swanson started helping his father in their family's small logging business when he was eleven. He remembered once when times were so hard that his dad could not afford to buy anything to grease the skids and Ted had to use water: "Gee it was a hot day and I had a yoke on my shoulders that had ropes down and hooks on it so I carried two five gallon cans of water with that yoke and up on a skid road and throw the water."[18] Ten gallons of water weigh eighty pounds—about as much as some eleven year olds weigh. Regardless of age or size, everyone in the logging camp worked hard.

Eight oxen were needed to pull this huge log over a skid road.

2

BUILDING THE FIRST TRANSCONTINENTAL RAILROAD

Railroads were introduced into the eastern United States in 1828. They spread quickly—more than 40,000 miles of railroad track had been laid by 1860. Regular train service, providing fast, year-round transportation of people, crops, and merchandise, began there during the 1850s. But not even one mile of track had been laid in the Oregon Territory by 1860, and only twenty-three miles laid in the entire state of California. Why? Did westerners not want the advantages of rail transportation?

"There are many and very important reasons requiring the construction of this great work [a transcontinental railroad]," resolved the Washington territorial legislature in 1858. "It will bind together this vast republic and be a chain of union between the Atlantic and Pacific states. It will insure the defense of the country. Armies, seamen, military and naval stores may be transported from ocean to ocean. . . . It will give a direct, quick transit to mails. Military reasons call for its construction. Political reasons require that it should be made; and more than all, commercial reasons demand it."[1] Clearly, western residents strongly desired railroads.

None had been built in the West in part because of the expense of transporting the equipment there. Everything other than lumber for railroad ties had to be either imported from England or built in America on the East Coast and shipped by boat. The iron equipment was far too heavy to be hauled thousands of miles across the continent by ox wagon.

The second reason there was no railroad development in the West was its small population. No private company could afford the great expense of building a railroad where

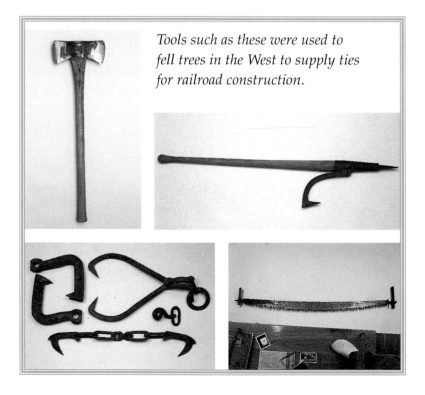

Tools such as these were used to fell trees in the West to supply ties for railroad construction.

there would be no paying passenger or freight traffic for several years. The help of the nation's government would be needed. However, the northern states and the slave-holding states could not agree where the route should go. The North did not want a railroad to help develop the Southwest, which would accept slavery. During the Civil War, Congress decided to build a railroad that would cross the continent from Nebraska to California, but actual construction had to wait until the war ended.

After the war, public sentiment rapidly developed in support of building the Pacific Railroad. Samuel Bowles's publication of a book describing his travels by stagecoach from the Missouri River to the Pacific Ocean in 1865 made the patriotic case for the railroads' ability to make the no-longer-divided nation a stronger one: "Men of the East! Men at Washington! You have given the toil and even the blood of a million of your brothers and fellows for four years, and spent three thousand million dollars, to rescue one section of the Republic from barbarism and from anarchy; and your triumph makes the cost cheap. Lend now a few thousand of men, and a hundred millions of money, to create a new Republic; to marry to the Nation of the Atlantic an equal if not greater Nation of the Pacific. . . . Here is payment of your great debt; here is wealth unbounded; here the commerce of the world; here the completion of a Republic that is continental; but you must come and take them with the Locomotive."[2]

Building the first transcontinental railroad was an enormous task. It had to cross nearly 2,000 miles, through high mountain ranges, wide rivers, and lonely desert lands. The winters were bitterly cold, and the summers hot. Water, trees, and other necessities were not available in many places. But two companies were organized to do the job. The Central Pacific started building in Sacramento and headed east. The Union Pacific went west from Omaha. Each was authorized to lay track until their lines met.

The Union Pacific "commenced operations at Omaha, then a small town, destitute alike of the skill necessary for the practical construction of such a public work, and destitute even of the mere manual force necessary," reported the *Boston Journal* in 1868, marveling at the difficulty of building a railroad from the edge of the civilized United States through the middle of nowhere. "Mechanics were needed, laborers were needed; if they were summoned from abroad, boarding places must be found, and some kind of homes extemporized. There were no shops in which and no tools with which to labor. Shovels, spades, picks, plows, axes and other implements were to be purchased in Chicago, Buffalo, Boston, New York or Philadelphia, wherever they could be found best in quality and cheapest in price, and transported to this new point of departure."[3] The absence of all materials and supplies was an almost overwhelming barrier.

"And here again was another obstacle to be contended with, for as yet no rail track had been laid nearer than about 150 miles of the east bank of the Missouri River. Over this distance, therefore, all men and materials had to be transported by the slow and expensive process of wagon trains," the *Journal* continued. "The engine [locomotive] . . . was thus carried in wagons from Des Moines, on the river of that name, that at the time being the only available means of getting it through." Although the Union Pacific had an easier time getting all its materials to the work site than did the Central Pacific, it was still no simple undertaking. As the paper observed, "Again, west of the Missouri River the country is almost entirely destitute of trees . . . the very ties on which the railroad has been constructed had to be cut in Michigan, Ohio, Pennsylvania and New York, and teamed over the country. . . ."[4]

Union Pacific workers were frequently attacked by Indian war parties of 20 to 200 warriors. United States Army General John Pope wrote to the War Department in 1865: "There is not a tribe on the great plains or in the mountain regions east of Nevada and Idaho but which is warring on the whites. The first demand of the Indian is that the white man shall not come into his country; shall not kill or drive off the game upon which his subsistence depends; and shall not dispossess him of his lands. How can we promise this, with any hope or purpose of fulfilling the obligation, unless we prohibit the immigration and settlement west of the Missouri River?"[5]

The railroad was the most visible symbol of white intrusion. During much of the construction period, every mile had to be surveyed and graded under army protection. The army assigned almost 30,000 men to guard the Union Pacific construction, including escorting supplies and equipment to the front in large wagon trains.

Arthur Ferguson was a surveyor for the Union Pacific, deciding where the railroad should go. He wrote in his diary on June 2, 1867: "This morning, shortly after sunrise the camp was aroused by the cry of here they come! here they come boys! and for the next few minutes the interior of our tent presented a lively picture—the soldiers, Mr. Boyd and myself grasping our arms, and regardless of our clothing and everything else we rushed out of the tent and there we saw the Indians charging down upon us from the

Indians resented railroad surveyors and workers who invaded Indian lands, so they attacked the workers to drive them off.

northern bluffs. . . ."[6] After their successful defense of the camp, he learned that all except one of the Union Pacific survey camps in a twenty-mile radius had been attacked that same morning. He was so worried about Indian attacks that he always slept with a rifle next to him, and a loaded revolver by his head. Surveyors and grading crews were the most at risk because they worked hundreds of miles ahead of the completed line.

Construction crews were in less danger because there were thousands of men working together, and they outnumbered the largest Indian raiding parties. Nonetheless, "federal troops guarded us, and we reconnoitered, surveyed, located and built inside of their picket line," wrote General Grenville Dodge, the chief construction engineer, in his memoirs. "We marched to work to the tap of the drum with our men armed. They stacked their arms on the dump and were ready at a moment's warning to fall in and fight for their territory."[7]

Because there had never been a railroad all the way across the country, the nation's newspapers wrote many stories about the construction as it occurred. Although few of the workers left written memoirs, journalists who traveled along reported in detail to their readers. Cy Warman was one reporter who shared the details of the daily life in a grading camp with the folks back east:

"The younger men are usually selected as drivers, the older for ploughing and filling, and the Irish for shovellers. A man with a good eye and an unmistakable accent is selected for the important job of dumping boss. He stands on the fill and indicates with his shovel where he wants the dirt dumped. Between teams he levels the dirt, and under his constant care the grade grows with just the proper pitch, until the top is levelled off ready for the cross ties . . . ,"[8] wrote Warman. Grading the roadbed to a level surface on which the ties and tracks would sit was the second stage of construction, after the surveyors had selected the best route.

Since the graders were operating in wilderness, sleeping accommodations and meals had to be provided for them as they proceeded across hundreds of miles of undeveloped country. Warman reported: "One of the first tents to go up is the hotel tent, and the man who runs it is the boarding boss. He is usually a jolly, fearless man, a good hustler, but not necessarily addicted to real manual toil. His wife does that. From four in the morning until midnight this slave of the camp is on her feet. To be sure, there are men cooks and flunkies and dishwashers, but the boarding boss has but one wife, and she must oversee everything."[9] She was the only woman on the grading crew.

"When the camp is established, the various bosses take their places and the work begins. The stable boss assigns men to the teams. He may have a hundred horses and mules, but he knows them all by name. Each man is personally responsible to the stable boss for the good care of his team."[10] Without horses the grading work would have been impossible. They pulled carts filled with dirt to and from the roadbed and dragged leveling equipment behind.

Once the soil had been graded, the construction crews followed. The *Chicago Tribune* reported in detail in 1867 what the workers actually did. "A couple of feet from the end of the rails already down, checks were placed under the wheels [of supply cars moved to the end of the most recently laid track], stopping the car at once. Before it had well stopped, a dozen men grasped a rail on each side, ran it beyond the car, laid it down . . . gauged it, and ere its clang in falling had ceased to reverberate, the car was run over it and another pair of rails drawn out."[11] Using the newly laid rails to bring more supplies forward was the most efficient way.

"This process was continued as rapidly as a man would walk. Behind the car followed a man dropping spikes, another setting the ties well under the ends of the rails, and thirty or forty others driving in the spikes and stamping the earth under the ties. The moment that one car was emptied of its iron, a number of men seized it and threw it off the track into the ditch, and the second followed on with its load. The work was all done with excessive rapidity, simply because each man had but a certain thing to do, was accustomed to doing it, and had not to wait on the action of any one else."[12] Mid-nineteenth-century readers were impressed with the degree of organization and efficiency with which the construction occurred.

When construction began, the only non-Indian settlements west of Omaha were a few army forts. New towns appeared practically overnight as the railroad came through lands previously unsettled by whites. The company set up many of them as sites for railroad repairs and housing for the men who worked on the trains. When Cheyenne, Wyoming, was mapped and subdivided by the railroad company on July 10, 1867, in the wilderness, the closest railroad track was 121 miles farther east. The first settlers arrived exactly one week later, well ahead of the tracks, and a tent village was put up. Two months later the town had a hundred saloons, two hotels, and a newspaper. The lack of law and order is suggested by the newspaper's daily column called "Last Night's Shootings." Likewise, the *Deseret News* of Salt Lake City, Utah, reported on March 28, 1869: "The place is fast becoming civilized, several men having been killed there already, the last one was found in the river with four bullet holes through him and his head badly mangled."[13]

Temporary settlements known as "hells on wheels" also sprang up at the end of the track, when the supply train brought the next shipment of supplies to build the track another few dozen miles. The towns moved with the men to the next work site. The construction crews were all men, and included many Civil War veterans and Irish immigrants. They were hundreds or thousands of miles from their families and civilized conditions. The absence of families, laws, and courts, and the presence of so many taverns and ways for drunken men to get into fights, made the railroad camps dangerous places, especially on payday.

Henry Stanley wrote about Julesburg, Colorado Territory, a typical end-of-the-line camp: "I verily believe that there are men here who would murder a fellow creature for five dollars. Nay, there are men who have already done it, and who stalk abroad in daylight unwhipped of justice. Not a day passes but a dead body is found somewhere in the vicinity with pockets rifled of their contents."[14] Places like Julesburg presented the Union Pacific workers with dangers not faced by the Central Pacific, with its largely Chinese workforce and a management that did not tolerate such establishments along the line.

"The Central Pacific Railroad Company advertises for 5,000 laborers to work upon the road between Newcastle and Illinoistown (Colfax)," announced the railroad in the *Shasta* (California) *Courier*, January 2, 1865. "It is the intention of the company to employ at once as many men as can be advantageously worked on the distance between these points—23 miles. The iron for laying this additional amount of track is already in Sacramento and it is expected that the cars will run to Illinoistown by August next. This opportunity affords a chance for those out of employment."[15] There was a shortage of workers because many men had been drafted for the Civil War, and others were working in the gold mines. To get enough workers and to speed construction, in 1865 the Central Pacific started hiring Chinese immigrants. They spoke no English and were unskilled in railroad construction. The chief engineer,

Mr. Strobridge, was prejudiced and initially unwilling to hire them.

Charles Crocker, a founder of the company, testified to the Pacific Railway Commission that he first recommended hiring Chinese workers when his Irish employees threatened to strike unless they got a wage increase. He said, "It was four or five months after that before I could get Mr. Strobridge to take Chinamen. Finally he took in fifty Chinamen, and a while after that he took in fifty more. Then, they did so well that he took fifty more, and he got

This Chinese work crew was among several crews laying track in 1868.

more and more until finally we got all we could use, until at one time I think we had ten or twelve thousand."[16]

E. B. Crocker, an investor in the railroad, wrote: "A large part of our force are Chinese and they . . . are far more reliable. No danger of strikes among them. We are training them to do all kinds of labor, blasting, driving horses, handling rock, as well as the pick and shovel."[17] The Chinese laborers were uncommonly hardworking and ingenious. One problem the railroad faced was the granite of the mountains called the Sierra Nevada. In some places the surface had to be leveled to lay track. The Chinese wove reeds into wicker baskets and lowered themselves hundreds of feet down the side of cliffs to bore holes in the rock. They stuffed the holes with dynamite and fuses and pulled themselves up before the explosion occurred.

In addition to blasting a roadbed on the sides of granite hills, the railroad needed thirteen tunnels dug through solid granite so hard that after a day's work the tunnel was not even a foot longer than the day before. Erle Heath, a historian for the Central Pacific, recorded that "with the exception of a few white men at the west end of tunnel No. 6, the laboring force was composed entirely of Chinese, with white foremen—the laborers working usually in three shifts of eight hours each, and the foremen in two shifts of twelve hours each."[18] Even with this intense level of effort, two years were required to get the track through the mountains.

Winter in the High Sierra, with its bitter cold, violent snowstorms, and frequent avalanches, was brutal for all the workers. Grading the roadbed had to be stopped when the snow arrived; only tunneling could continue. Deaths due to weather conditions were common. When John Gillis worked in the mountains in the winter of 1866–1867, snow-storms "were so frequent across the trail leading to tunnel No. 9 that it had to be abandoned for some months. At tunnel 10 some fifteen or twenty Chinese were killed by a slide at about this time,"[19] he reported.

The Chinese laborers worked in all-Chinese crews with a Chinese headman and a Chinese cook. Eating a Chinese diet and drinking tea kept them healthier than the white workers who drank water, because boiling the water to brew tea killed illness-causing bacteria in the water.

A Chinese "tea man" carried tea to the Chinese work crews several times a day.

Most Chinese workers lived frugally, saving their money to send back to their families in China. When the Central Pacific was finished and offered no more construction work, they scattered and helped build railroads in other parts of the country before immigration laws were changed to exclude them.

The first transcontinental railroad was completed in May 1869, when the tracks of the Central Pacific and Union Pacific railroads converged at Promontory, Utah. A golden spike was pounded in to mark the spot where they met. The grueling venture had injured or killed thousands of pioneer railroad workers, but they had created a connection that rapidly developed the United States.

A typical early locomotive

3

THE RAILROADS EXPAND

The completion of the Union Pacific/Central Pacific railroad marked the beginning of a western railroad building boom that would last another forty years. The early local railroads were primitive, as John Murphy's experiences in the 1870s suggest:

"I was placed on some iron in an open truck and told to cling to the sides, and to be careful not to stand on the wooden floor if I cared anything about my limbs. I promised a strict compliance with the instructions, and the miserable little engine gave a grunt or two, several wheezy puffs, a cat-like scream, and finally got the car attached to it under way. Once in motion, it dashed on at a headlong speed of two miles an hour . . . and at the end of seven hours hauled one weary passenger, with eyes made sore from the smoke, and coat and hat nearly burnt off by the sparks, into a station composed of a rude board shanty, through whose apertures the wind howled, having made the entire distance of fifteen miles in that time."[1]

Murphy was an Englishman visiting the Pacific

Northwest soon after the Walla Walla & Columbia River Railroad was completed. The Walla Walla wheat farmers had decided to build a small railroad from the river to the town in 1871 because the local teamsters' charges to haul the grain by wagon were too high and reduced the farmers' profits too much. It was a do-it-yourself operation; the company's president—who also served as its secretary, conductor, brakeman, and ticket seller—selected the route, rafted logs from Idaho, sawed them in his steam mill, and supervised all the construction. The first ten miles of road were built entirely of wood—the rails as well as the ties. When it was completed, the railroad charged less than half what the wagon teamsters charged. Many comparable local "short lines" were built in the West, for settlers wanted faster, more dependable, and, above all, cheaper transportation.

Additional transcontinental lines were also built—the Northern Pacific, the Great Northern, the Santa Fe, and others. Railroad builders encountered rugged conditions as they pioneered the new routes. D. C. Linsley wrote in his journal of starting his journey to locate a usable pass

Lumber could be bound into a boat-shaped raft to move the lumber on a river.

through the Cascade Mountains in 1870: "We had two canoes and three weeks rations of flour, bacon and tea. With the Exception of our instruments and blankets we carried nothing else."[2]

Nineteen years later, things were not much easier for John Stevens. "Buying some old snowshoe frames from the Indians, I patched up something that resembled snowshoes, which I knew would be needed," wrote the civil engineer of his experience surveying for a Great Northern Railway pass through the Rockies in Montana in December 1889. "We were able to use the mule team nearly to the foot of the mountains, stopping at night in abandoned Indian cabins. When the deepening snow prevented further progress with the team, I sent it back to the last cabin with orders to remain there until my return, and we pushed on afoot with some food and our blankets."[3]

Because Stevens found the lowest northern pass in the Continental Divide the Great Northern Railway could cross the Rockies without having to build a tunnel. He never forgot the dangerous evening he had to spend there in -40°F weather to confirm his discovery. "There was no possibility of making a fire with nothing but green brush and evergreens showing above the deep snow," he wrote. "So I tramped a path until the snow would bear me without snowshoes, and walked it back and forth until the first streak of daylight. I had some bread and bacon, both frozen, and did not suffer from hunger. Had I not kept moving I would have frozen to death."[4]

Even though twenty-five years had passed since the Union Pacific had first pushed through the country hundreds of miles to the south, conditions were still primitive in undeveloped areas. Even shortly before World War I, Joseph Noble, surveying for the Santa Fe Railroad, wrote:

"A surveying party working in this country had to operate a good deal like an exploring expedition in the days of Coronado."[5] (Francisco Vásquez de Coronado was a Spaniard who explored the American Southwest in the 1540s.) Surveying parties lived in tents—even in a blizzard—and ate whatever did not need refrigeration.

In 1881 Charlie Prescott, a machinist, decided to go to Montana, where the new Northern Pacific Railroad was under construction. "I engaged passage on a mule team train to Billings, Mont.," he recalled in his memoirs. "In covering 500 miles through a rough and new country, it was necessary to build a raft of logs to ferry Powder River on account of the spring rise. We passed in sight of the Custer battlefield on the Little Big Horn River, and were nearly one month making the trip. . . ."[6]

Until the railroads were completed, any journey like Prescott's through the wilderness was slow. The Indian troubles that had delayed the Union Pacific's construction were still in recent memory, as his reference to the famous battle suggests, but Indian resistance was no longer a threat.

"We arrived at Carlson, Mont., adjoining the new town of Billings. It was one big storehouse built by the Northern Pacific. A lot of board shacks and tents made up the town. The track had been laid only as far as the Big Horn River, 50 miles east. I concluded I'd remain and get a job as a machinist, as a shop terminal was to be located [at Billings] on arrival of the track," Prescott related. "Rails were being laid about a mile a day; the track arrived about two months after [I did]. . . ."[7]

As each new railroad moved across the country, it created towns and jobs from the wilderness that lay along the way, just as the Union Pacific had done. All railroads created a series of division headquarters along the line, where machinery repairs could be performed and where men who served on the train trips would stay between runs. Wherever any railroad decided to locate the round-house and other facilities, new towns were quickly settled. Where there were railroads to bring and haul away goods, and railroad workers with paychecks to spend, was a good place for others to set up business.

Before the railroad arrived, Prescott ran a steam engine sawing bridge timbers for the railroad's crossing of the Yellowstone River near Billings. The 1880s were a time when steam engines were being adapted to supply power for many different activities in addition to powering rail-road locomotives. It was easy for a skilled mechanic to find work on different machines, but working for the railroad was the most prestigious occupation. Therefore, recalled Prescott, "I soon landed the job as the first machinist in

A roundhouse was a place where train engines and cars were repaired. Roundhouses were stationed at intervals along railroads.

Billings. . . . The town was growing very fast in 1883. . . .
The railroad soon built a boarding house, called The
Beanery, for employees. . . . [The beds] were wooden bunks
filled with straw. I had buffalo robes to sleep under,"[8]

Life in the early railroad towns may have seemed
rough to Charlie Prescott, but living conditions were often
truly primitive for the section gangs. Kaneo Kawahara,
who immigrated from Japan and got a job on the Great
Northern in Montana in 1899 at the age of seventeen, hated
the conditions. Montana seemed to him "an utter waste-
land. As for drinking water, once a week a flat-car came
carrying a huge storage tank of water. Water was the most
precious thing, and we never used it for bathing. All
we could do was to wipe off our sweat with the least
amount of water possible. In summertime, inside the tank,
mosquito larvae bred prolifically. Since we had no bath tub,
whenever a rain came, no matter what we were doing or
where we were, we jerked off our clothes and had a natural
shower."[9]

Everyone experienced the isolation of frontier conditions to some extent, but it was particularly hard for
non-English-speaking immigrants. Kawahara wrote about
the lonely life of Japanese in a section gang: "There were
twenty-four workers on the section, among whom hardly
anyone understood English. We waited for the Tobo man
[employment broker] to come three or four times a year to
state our requests and demands through him. . . . Those
who were killed or injured at work by running trains were
carried away on that same train. Even if we asked the foreman whether they were hospitalized and got proper treat-
ment or whether they died on the way, our English was not
understood, and neither could we understand the answer.
It was miserable."[10]

44

Though few men left written recollections, thousands shared similar experiences of working on a frontier railroad. During the 1880s almost 100,000 miles of railroad track were laid and new train services was established in the West. In 1880 there were some 400,000 railroaders in America; in 1889 more than 700,000 were employed.

The railroads' need for timber for railroad ties, bridges, and company buildings also created many opportunities for men to log and run sawmills along the route. Kenneth Forbes Ross arrived in Montana as a teenager in the 1880s and went to work for a company that had two sawmills and a contract to provide bridge timbers to the Northern Pacific, then under construction. When the supervisor of one of the mills quit suddenly, Ross was put in charge, at the age of twenty, of managing the company's logging, lumber manufacture, and hiring.

"After the timber was pretty well cut out around the mill I had charge of," he wrote, "I was instructed to move it to Bonner, and set it up for the purpose of cutting out lumber for a dam, bunkhouse, buildings, and for timbers for a sawmill they contemplated constructing."[11] This practice was very common in the lumber industry; the sawmills were moved again and again, to remain close to the timber as it was cut farther back.

"I decided to try and get into the lumber business for myself, so I purchased a little sawmill . . . which had a capacity of about 25,000 feet a day. My brother George, being an engineer, went into a partnership with me, and we moved our little mill. . . . The Montana Central Railroad was just starting to build from Helena to Butte. . . . I secured a contract to furnish bridge timbers."[12] In the 1880s it was still possible to start a small lumbermill without much money.

4

WORKING FOR
THE RAILROAD

What did railroad workers do, and how did they learn the necessary skills? A complex business such as a railroad had scores of different activities. Driving the engine was as different from operating the telegraph as it was from repairing damaged track or repainting the inside of a passenger car. Some jobs were unique to the railroads; others used skills shared by different occupations. The skills also changed over time as new equipment was developed.

Some railroading job skills could be gained only from experience on the trains themselves. This was especially true of jobs in the "running trades"—the locomotive engineer, who operated the engine; the fireman, who kept the engine stoked with fuel; the conductor, who was in charge of the train and the passengers; and the brakeman, who slowed the train down by operating brakes on top of each car. Although these jobs made up only 20 percent of the work force, the people in these jobs suffered more than half the deaths and injuries.

August Shaw started working as a brakeman near the end of the Civil War. In 1890 he described his work setting brakes car by car in these words: "During cold weather we go into the caboose occasionally to warm ourselves. We are called out by a signal of 'down brakes.' We get out on top of the train. We find that the top of the cars are completely covered with sleet. In attempting to get at those brakes a great many brakemen lose their lives, slip off the cars and again, even if they do reach the brakes . . . [often] they find that the brakes are frozen up, and they cannot twist them. . . . As no brakes are set, all will depend on the engine to stop the train, and if the train was going with any speed it would take some time to stop it."[1]

For such dangerous work special qualities were needed. Dick Nelson, a freight brakeman in Wyoming during the 1870s, described them: "That took nerve, coordination, timing, and a perfect sense of balance, to go over the top of a freight train—winter or summer. . . . Rain, snow, sleet, ice all over the roofs and on brake wheels and handholds."[2]

Brakemen probably had the two riskiest jobs on the train. In addition to setting the brakes, brakemen also had the task of connecting cars to each other. Nelson describes why so many brakemen in the early days had missing fingers and hands: "Judge the speed of the moving car coming toward you. Lift the link so it will enter the pocket of the draw bar. Get hands and fingers out of the way—you may need 'em some time. Damage to the equipment will result if the link goes over or under the pocket. Then you'll have to go back to the [caboose], loop a bull-chain around your neck, come back, get that crippled car out of the train and onto a side track. Then get ready to catch hell from the boss because you've been so clumsy. If you'd really been

In the early days of rail-roading, the brake on each car had to be set by hand.

clumsy and stepped under the wheels of a moving car, you'd wind up dead, or crippled for life."[3] In fact, one of every six deaths of railway workers resulted from coupling or uncoupling trains. Federal safety laws did not require the companies to use automatic couplers or air brakes until 1893.

The locomotive engineer actually ran the train. He made sure there was correct steam pressure and that the other machinery was in good working order and was operating properly. Steam pressure turned the wheels; to get proper pressure, the firebox had to be the right temperature, and there had to be enough water in the boiler. Too much pressure was dangerous, and too little pressure would not provide enough power to move the train. The engineer was also the driver, judging the right speed, how long it would take to stop, and the conditions of the track.

Henry Clay French shared with his son stories of his railroad service from 1873 to 1930. He started working as a messenger boy at age thirteen, and had eight different jobs in his career on the railroads. "Having been a conductor, and now being an engineer, I had plenty of ground for a definite comparison of the two jobs," he said. "I must admit that, from the engineer's seat box, the job of conductor seemed to me to hold a number of advantages. The danger incident to the engineer's job was the only real incentive to remain in [the driver's seat],"[4] he joked.

The dangers were no joke. Train derailments and crashes were not uncommon in the nineteenth century and accounted for approximately one in seven railroad deaths. Of course, everyone else on the train shared the same danger as the engineer; they all counted on him to avoid it for

A locomotive engineer had the best-paying job on the railroad.

them. There are frequent accounts of engineers uncoupling the cars they pulled when they saw unavoidable danger coming. Mr. French's preference for being the conductor was unusual. Most men would have preferred the job of locomotive engineer, which was the best-paid, most prestigious, and most glamorous railroad occupation.

French's last derailment in the driver's seat was what prompted him to hang up his engineer's cap. When the chain on the tank brake broke as the train was coming down a steep hill, he did everything he could with the gears to slow the train down, without success. All the trainmen jumped off the speeding engine to avoid being killed. The engine jumped off the track into a hay field a mile past the bottom of the hill. French described his emotions thus: "No longer was she my beloved engine. I felt like kicking that pile of smoking metal for taking the glamour out of the job of the locomotive engineer. I knew that I had all the glory I wanted until some future time when there were better brakes on the engines themselves."[5]

The fireman's job was to keep fuel always burning in the firebox so that a constant temperature would be maintained. One old-time railroader used to watch the trains go by when he was a young man hoeing corn on hot summer days. Every time a train went by, he saw the men in the engine leaning out the windows watching the scenery. Because it seemed easier than farming, the youngster decided to become a fireman himself. But he quickly changed his mind: "I hadn't made more than two trips until I found out that that fireman wasn't leaning out the window looking at the scenery. He was hanging out there gasping for breath."[6] Typically, a fireman would shovel five tons or more of coal a day. The steeper the hill, the more power was needed, and the more fuel had to be added.

This 1910 locomotive was derailed by an avalanche. The track has been cleared, but the heavy locomotive still has not been put back on the rails.

Other jobs also had to be done to keep the railroads running. Men with a variety of skills kept the engines and cars in safe condition. This required boilermakers, machinists like Charlie Prescott, painters, blacksmiths, and other craftsmen. Some served a formal apprenticeship, as Charlie Prescott did beginning in 1873. He wrote, "At the age of 18, on finishing a term at Worcester Academy [Massachusetts], I made application by letter to the Mason Locomotive Works at Taunton, Mass., for an apprenticeship to learn the machinist trade."[7] The president of the company wrote back, offering him a three-year training, starting at 80¢ a day the first year, for 285 days of work each year, which he accepted. After his training, Prescott was qualified to build and repair the enormous steam locomotives.

College training was desirable in a few professions, such as civil engineering. Grenville Dodge, who became the chief engineer of the Union Pacific, trained as a civil and military engineer at an eastern university. But there were some distinguished engineers who did not have that kind of technical training. John Stevens, who not only was the engineer for the Great Northern Railroad but also helped design and construct the Panama Canal, developed

John Stevens is shown here next to a monument commemorating his discovery of the shortest route to the Pacific Northwest thirty-six years before.

his career by reading engineering books while gaining practical experience in the field.

Some jobs used skills that were transferable to and from other occupations. Stations along the track hired people to sell tickets, handle baggage, unload freight, send and receive telegrams, and schedule the trains to move at safe distances from each other.

Not all jobs were open to all people. African-American workers were segregated into a limited number of job openings. Some worked as railroad laborers, but almost their only opportunity in the trains themselves was in Pullman porter service.

Pullman porters were sleeping-car attendants who made up the beds and generally looked after sleeping-car passengers. Almost all the porters were African-American. They learned the basics in a sleeping car on a side track at the Pullman factory in Chicago. Then they served as apprentices on regular runs until they received their own assignment. The western runs created a problem for the Pullman porters that did not exist in the more civilized East, such as persuading cowboys and miners to remove their boots before getting into the sleeping berths. One porter recalled: "They wanted to keep them on. They seemed afraid to take them off."[8]

Likewise, very few foreign-born men were ever employed in the running trades. Partly because of their limited English, a large number were hired only for manual labor, both during construction and for section work later. Many Swedish men worked for the Great Northern, and then came Italians, as well as Irish tracklayers.

After construction, every mile of track on every system had to be examined frequently by section gangs. If

The occupation of Pullman porter was one of the few available on the railroads to African Americans.

roadbeds were not reinforced, if worn-out ties were not replaced, if loose pins were not pounded back in, if obstacles were not removed from the rails, trains could derail, killing or injuring many people.

In the 1890s and early 1900s railroad work became one of the primary sources of employment for Japanese immigrants. The 1900 census showed that more than one of every four Japanese males worked as steam railroad employees, principally as laborers.

Inota Tawa was recruited by a Japanese employment broker to work in Idaho in 1893 to complete the building of the Great Northern Railroad. The contractor wanted his workers to live like Americans. Mr. Tawa remembered: "The employment broker wouldn't let us use miso soup, soy sauce, or rice in the camps. Chinese wore a long queue wound up on top of their heads and were dressed in long-trained Chinese robes. We dressed like American railroad workers in shirts and dungarees and American shoes. Chinese seemed to have the custom of eating warm rice three times a day . . . we Japanese were not supposed to eat rice, and so we had many strange menus. Since bread was expensive and we could not afford the same food as whites, we ate dumpling soup for breakfast and supper. . . ."[9]

Although the Japanese were supposed to live like Americans, they were not paid like Americans. Mr. Tawa and the other Japanese in his crew earned $1.15 for working a ten-hour day, with 10¢ subtracted for the broker's employment commission. American workers were paid $1.45 for the same day's work.

Kichisaburo Ishimitsu found work soon after arriving in the United States. "I joined a Great Northern gang which was working near a tunnel on the other side of the Cascade Mountains. Our job was to change the rails and ties inside the tunnel. Six of us in two rows lifted the 40-foot rails, using levers. . . . We made $1.35 a day for ten hours of work."[10]

Working conditions and living conditions were both rather primitive, so there was a steady turnover of workers. The graders did not like living in tents and the tracklayers disliked the crowded, dormitorylike railroad cars. Kichisaburo Ishimitsu recorded: "We slept in double-decked bunks in a freight car, in the center of which was a coal stove."[11] During harvest season men easily found other jobs harvesting the crops, so new workers were always sought.

In regions where large amounts of snow buried the tracks, routine maintenance could not occur during winter. The tracks were cleared of snow to allow the trains through, but nothing more. Inota Tawa recalled that as they were unskilled laborers, "Two or three months every winter we were out of a job. Those who made satisfactory work record could remain in the same section camp, but others were sent into an isolated winter camp . . . until the snow melted in spring."[12] This prevented unhappy workers from leaving the region.

Some of the construction workers were single men who moved from one construction job to the next. They did not have stable homes or families and were called "boomers." But many of the construction workers were men who were only doing railroad work temporarily to save enough money to move into what they really wanted to do. Often, people who moved west to farm did not have enough money to survive until their first crop was planted, grown, and sold. They worked on the railroad just long enough to acquire the needed money and then quit to farm.

Because of both language difficulties and homesickness, people tended to stick together with others from the same background and to follow their old customs. Isuke Miyazaki, a Great Northern employee, recalled that each group tried to fix its national foods as best it could. "I remember that Italians working in the same gang were baking bread in a special way. They made the ovens by digging holes in the wall of a steep cliff by the railway. They burned thousands of old railroad ties to make the fire hot enough, and used the ovens for baking bread. Sometimes they gave me some. It was crusty French-style bread. They baked enough for ten days at one time. They also cooked Italian macaroni stews."[13]

Miyazaki's Japanese work crew, by contrast, ate Japanese rice with tomato soup. Many Japanese immigrants saved their money to send to their families in Japan and spent as little as possible on food. As a result, the workers often developed night blindness from malnutrition. It disappeared when they learned to supplement their diet, but before that, night blindness was particularly severe among teenage boys, whose bodies were still growing.

Harmony was more common among the different nationalities working for the railroad than it was with nearby white communities. For example, relations between Japanese camps and white towns were sometimes violent. Jinzo Ekumi's uncle was working on a railroad section in Oregon when shots were fired into his sleeping quarters. Ekumi wrote: "Later it was revealed that the rioters were neighboring poor farmers. They had worked on railroad sections during their off-season and, seeing the six foreigners there, they were afraid their livelihoods would be in danger after that. So they plotted the attack. My uncle and the others hastily got their belongings together and left the very next day."[14] This was inconvenient both for the railroad, which had to hire new workers, and the labor contractor, who lost his daily commission from each worker.

Where were the women? Railroading was a man's job. Practically no women worked in the railroad industry. The exceptions were the Harvey Girls and a few widows. Harvey Girls were waitresses in Fred Harvey's chain of restaurants along the Santa Fe line. He was the first to employ women in that capacity. The widows were typically women in small stations who were allowed by the railroads to continue in some nonphysical jobs after their husbands died. Many railroad wives in such places took in railroad workers as roomers and boarders, but since the wives were not employed by the railroads, no one considered them railroaders.

5

LOGGING AFTER 1880

Attie Long, the daughter of the pioneer logger in the first chapter, remembers how her father turned to a different way of supporting his family: "When Pa wasn't using the oxen he turned them out and they grazed close to the house. One day during a sudden thunderstorm one of the oxen was struck by lightning, almost in our yard, and this ended Pa's logging."[1]

If David Long had started logging ten years later, the lightning would not have ended his logging career. In 1881 John Dolbeer invented a steam-powered machine that soon replaced bull teams in logging. Dolbeer had come west from New Hampshire in 1850 to look for gold and eventually became a sawmill owner. He invented a small, high-pressure steam engine that, by turning a rope through sets of gears, hauled in heavy logs tied to the other end of the rope. This "donkey engine" was more powerful than oxen, did not eat, and never tired out. If fed a constant supply of wood and water, it could produce steam forever.

At first the donkey engine was just used to haul logs from where they fell to the skid road. This was called "yarding." After steel-wire cable was invented, several donkey engines could be placed along the skid road, and the logs could be hauled from engine to engine. Thereafter oxen were not needed.

Although bullwhackers lost their jobs, the steam engine created jobs for more men. A donkey engine could yard so many more logs in a day than oxen that more men's wages could be paid with the money from the additional logs. Now each man did one task all day. The splitter chopped wood for the fire that boiled the water into steam. The fireman stoked the firebox. Still another man had to keep the right amount of water in the boiler, and Bill

The Shay-type donkey engine was used in Seattle around 1891 to haul logs.

Bighill's first job was "hauling water for a steam donkey with a horse. I would pump it down and then I'd have to pump it up on the top of the hill into a barrel and haul it to the donkey and then dump it into a tank and keep that up all day. I was getting a horse and getting a dollar a day."[2]

Chokermen crawled under felled trees to hook them up to the steel cables. The puncher managed the rigging lines attached to the big logs being dragged to the donkey yard. He was told not to tighten the main line until there was a whistle signal. A whistle punk like Frank McKinnon blew the steam whistle that let workers out of sight of the engine know that the logs were about to start or stop moving. "One [blast of the whistle] was stop or go . . . two . . . was bring [the lines] back out. And three was go ahead slow. And four, they wanted the foreman,"[3] he wrote. Men hated to hear four blasts in a row, for it frequently meant that one of their fellow workers had been injured or killed on the job, so the foreman was being summoned. This sometimes resulted when a tree limb accidentally fell on the whistle wire, which gave the go signal. When the puncher started the power, the moving log would crush anyone in its way.

Steam donkeys were used on the forest floor. An alternative way to get logs to the mill was to float them instead of dragging them. Timber was abundant near the white-water rivers in the western mountains. Seasonal workers called "river pigs" were employed to drive the logs all the way down the mountain to the sawmills at the bottom. The drives occurred only in the spring, when melting snow filled the rivers to their highest level.

River pigs had to balance on floating logs and break up the logjams. Bert Wilke, a river pig himself, described

A logjam such as this one could be dangerous and difficult to break up.

this dangerous work: "When you're on the rear of a drive you pull logs with your pike pole out into the main stream from where they're caught in the brush. You sack the logs in and keep 'em floating. From the upper end you'd clean the stream as you'd go down, working on logs all the time. . . . One day about twenty of us were working on the front end of the jam. The logs were piled up thirty feet high and there was not even enough water to get your feet wet. All of the water was in back and when that force started to move the jam there was nothing to stop it."[4]

Wilke recalled a fellow river pig who jumped the wrong way when a logjam broke and let loose all the water that had been held back: "If he'd have jumped and angled toward shore and kept his feet, the water wasn't too deep, he could probably have stayed on his feet and got out. But he didn't, and he rode down and the last we seen of him he was in between two logs when he went down around the curve. You couldn't keep up with him. They never found nothin' of him."[5]

Frank Kordes admired the toughness of the river pigs he worked with: "I have seen men to their neck in water with ice floating right along side of them. What held them up I don't know. . . . I don't think a man nowadays would be able to take it . . . couldn't begin to. They had heavy wool underwear on, heavy wool clothes, out in the water all day up to their necks. At night, I was told, that they would go to bed [wet] . . . they never dried their clothes out because if they did they would just be doing the same thing in the morning."[6]

Logging work around the turn of the century was so strenuous that the men needed to eat huge meals—about 8,000 calories daily—to be able to work a ten-hour shift. Logging camps usually provided three sit-down meals a day. The same food was served for breakfast, lunch, and dinner. A typical menu would include hot meats, baked beans, potatoes, biscuits, pancakes, and coffee. Often the cook would add variety with vegetables and desserts. One timber company statistician wrote that every day a 1,000-man crew would eat 1,000 pounds of fresh meat, 200 pounds of smoked meat, a ton of fresh fruits and vegetables, 900 pounds of flour, 600 pounds of sugar, 190 pounds of butter, and almost 3,000 eggs, plus coffee, tea, and milk.

All the camps, whatever their size, had a no-talking rule at the table. Bert Wilke explained it: "You didn't dare talk around them old camp cooks. They'd shut you up in a hurry . . . you could ask someone to pass something but that was all."[7] One explanation was that if the men didn't talk to each other, they would be less likely to get into a fight at the table. Another rationale was that the cooks

Large meals in a logging camp in the 1880s were served three times a day.

didn't want to hear any complaints about their cooking! Bert Wilke simply said that "some of them old cooks, they got pretty mean."[8]

That meanness may have resulted from how hard the logging camp cook's job was. Preparing and cleaning up after three huge hot meals a day, without refrigeration or sanitation, was grinding labor. But it was said to be the most important job in the camp. Frank McKinnon, a logger who worked in many different camps in the 1900s, recalled: "Once in a while, you'd get into a camp that wasn't too good. But you didn't stay there, I'll tell you that. You moved on, or they moved the cook, one of the two."[9] Bert Wilke, recalling his employment with the Baker Brothers Company before World War I, agreed: "When men were hard to get, all the Bakers had to do was hire their old cook,

George Helders. He was one of the best camp cooks in the country. All they had to do was hire him and all the lumberjacks they wanted would flock to where the best grub was."[10]

A hired logger could count on working long hours, facing danger in the course of his daily work, and enduring dirty, unpleasant working and living conditions. Everyone knew that life in a logging camp would be rougher than living in town because the camps were not permanent; when the nearby timber was cut out, the whole camp was moved to a fresh stand of trees. But the men, who paid for their meals and sleeping quarters by deductions from their wages, were resentful that the conditions were worse than they needed to be.

"At that time, why, all the lumberjacks carried their own beds and those camps'd get fulla bedbugs and lice," Bert Wilke described the unpleasant conditions of the smaller camps. "Men would pack 'em from one camp to another. You could build a new camp but before a month it would be lousy. You just had to put up with them. A lotta guys would mix powder in with their blankets to keep the bedbugs from keeping 'em awake. . . . Beds were hay to spread their blanket on."[11]

Peter Jaspers likewise vividly remembered that during the pre-World War I years, "we had to carry our own blankets. There was no bathrooms, no way to take a bath, only a creek or the river in them early days. There was no such. I worked in one place where they didn't have a toilet, you went out there by golly out in the woods. . . . And before, there was no [bed]springs and just boards."[12]

Frank Kordes remembered all the dirt. "The bunk houses weren't too good at that time, they were generally tent camps. Some of them were like being in a barn. . . .

Loggers in a typical bunkhouse, around 1910

They had smallpox in the spring of the year. The mud was about an inch thick in all the bunk houses, you couldn't keep it out. . . ."[13]

Conditions were poor in the logging camps in respects other than filthy mattresses, no place to bathe, and having to carry one's bedding in a "bindle." Few facilities for washing clothes existed. The heating of the living quarters was poor, and it was difficult to dry the work clothes that got drenched as the men worked in the frequent rains.

The Industrial Workers of the World tried to organize loggers into a union to improve their lives. Organized in 1905, the IWW wanted the companies to provide decent facilities: steel cots, clean bedding, mattresses, places to take baths and wash clothes, and sanitary food. A World

War I-era folksong summed up the men's conditions and
their feelings about them:

> Fifty thousand lumberjacks, fifty thousand
>   packs,
> Fifty thousand dirty rolls of blankets on their
>   backs,
> Fifty thousand minds made up to strike and
>   strike like men,
> For fifty years they've packed a bed, but never
>   will again.
>
> Fifty thousand wood bunks full of things that
>   crawl;
> Fifty thousand restless men have left them once
>   for all.
> One by one they dared not say, "Fat, the hours
>   are long."
> If they did, they'd hike—but now they're fifty
>   thousand strong.
>
> Fatty Rich, we know your game, know your
>   pride is pricked.
> Say—but why not be a man, and own when you
>   are licked?
> They've joined the One Big Union—Gee! For
>   goodness' sake,
> "Get wise!"
> The more you try to buck them now, the more
>   they organize.
>
>   —"Fifty Thousand Lumberjacks"[14]

There were 295 IWW-supported strikes in the lumber industry in 1917. George Hunsby recalled one of the more colorful protests in the "big movement to get better living conditions in the logging camps . . . they set one particular day as blanket burning day. . . . And there was hundreds of 'em came with their bundle rolls, you know, their dirty blankets and they had great big bonfires and they burned 'em all up."[15] When the United States entered World War I, the IWW protest cut production to 15 percent of normal in the Pacific Northwest. Because the lumber owners were able to convince the federal government that spruce trees used to build airplanes for the war were vital to the war effort, 27,000 soldiers were put to work in the lumber camps. Their presence led to the reforms that the IWW had wanted: an eight-hour day, shower facilities, and clean bunkhouses.

Although living conditions improved, nothing could change the working conditions. The western forests were very wet, with a great deal of rainfall, soggy ground, and moisture dripping from the trees even when the rain had passed. To stay dry, fallers in the West wore pants made of strong canvas dipped in hot paraffin wax to make them waterproof. They were called "tin pants" because they were so stiff and resisted snags from broken tree limbs and underbrush that would otherwise injure the loggers. They were held up by elastic suspenders. Joseph Stoneburg, a northwest logger, remembered: "They were awkward darn things to try and walk in, man, they were fierce! But in the wet climate you needed something like that for protection."[16] The faller might wear a shirt and a waterproof coat and hat, but the effort of felling a tree always stripped him down above the waist to his gray woolen underwear.

When he didn't wear his waterproof garments, he keenly felt the absense of a place to dry out his things.

Logging by its very nature was hard physical labor. In the West it took four men to cut down a tree. Two undercutters did the preliminary ax work; then two men working with a two-handled saw that was ten feet long were needed to bring the tree down. A big Douglas fir could occupy two men sawing for an entire day; a California redwood twenty to twenty-five feet around could take two men a week to cut down. As Sam Churchill described his working conditions, "You work in mud, rain and cold in winter, and you sweat to death and choke in your own dust in summer."[17]

A huge California redwood is dragged to the sawmill with the help of chains.

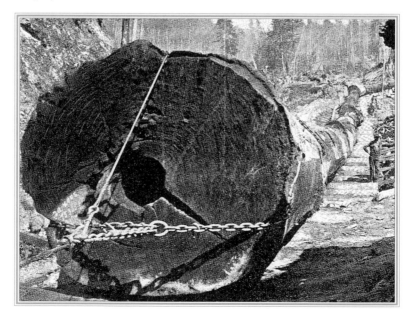

The men worked from sunrise to sunset six days a week, with only Sundays off. The Fourth of July and Christmas were the sole holidays. Everyone was expected to work hard, and men who didn't work hard were fired. "We got a dollar a day and board. For ten hours' work," Peter Jaspers recalled. "And you had to work too, boy, or else there was somebody to take your place."[18]

"Nobody ever pushed ya [to work faster]. Everybody worked then," George Hunsby put it. "Of course, they knew doggoned well if they didn't work they'd get canned. And, if they got canned, there was no place . . . no union to go back on to help you out. There was no unemployment compensation. There was no nothing, period. Your next move would be to get another job."[19]

Mr. Jaspers's boss even had a rule against men smoking cigarettes. He was not worried about the risk of causing a fire, nor about the workers' health. Jaspers recalled: "If a man would be smoking cigarettes he couldn't get a job . . . took too much time to roll a cigarette. . . . They wasn't going to pay men for rolling cigarettes, when there was work to be done."[20] Liquor was also forbidden in the camps.

This need to have everyone working hard resulted in part from the economics of logging as big business. In the 1890s large numbers of midwestern lumbermen, looking for more trees and new forests to cut after exhausting the midwestern white pine forests, had ridden the new Northern Pacific and Great Northern railroads from Michigan, Wisconsin, and Minnesota. When they saw that thickly forested northwest timberland was available cheaply, midwestern lumber businessmen began relocating to the West. They bought hundreds of thousands of acres from the railroads, which had been given the land by

Congress to help pay the costs of constructing the railroads. New machinery was needed to cut the huge acreages, and it was necessary to harvest a lot of timber to pay for it.

A technique called "high-lead logging" was developed to speed up the rate at which trees could be harvested. The highest tree was selected for the "spar," or pole to which all the rigging cables, ropes, and pulleys were attached. When other trees were cut down, those lines would be attached to them, and they would be lifted up in the air by the pulleys and swung far away. Because there was no friction in the air to slow down the logs, they moved much faster than on skid roads.

The high rigger's job was climbing the spar tree and preparing it. Bill Bighill, an old-time high rigger, said the biggest spar tree he ever climbed "was about nine feet in diameter, I cut off, I measured that one, cut the top off at two hundred feet, two hundred feet off the ground . . . it would take me quite a while, a lot of big limbs . . . the bigger the tree the harder it is to climb."[21] Joseph Stoneburg explained, "Had to take the branches off as you go up,"[22] because they climbed by circling the trunk with a rope tied to their belt, digging their spurs into the bark of the tree, hitching the rope another few feet, resetting their spurs, and continuing until they reached the top. That meant climbing with an ax and a saw, as well as the rope.

"When you got up to the necessary height, which was usually 200 to 210 feet, you put in a notch or undercut," Bighill explained, and removed only the top to attach the tackle. Then the rigger hung on tight, because when the top of the tree broke and started to fall, "it would make a couple of swings . . . and then it starts going in a circle,"[23] 200 feet up in the air.

A high rigger, shown here on top of a tall tree, had a particularly dangerous job in logging.

Logging had always been dangerous. It was said a man's life expectancy in the woods was no more than seven years. The worker might be crushed by a falling tree, or cut by his saw or ax and either bleed to death or die of blood poisoning. He might be run over by a log that fell off a load. He could drown riding logs down a river, or fall out of a tree. A steam engine or boiler could explode. Or high riggers could be shot into the air by the velocity of the swaying trunk.

The more advanced the technology became, the more ways there seemed to be for men to hurt themselves and one another. The men who climbed the high trees to rig up pulleys and cables faced new dangers. Mr. Stoneburg told about the one that frightened him the most, 200 feet up in the air, sawing the undercut to top the tree: "You better get those corners so that they are going to break when that top starts to go. If you don't, you're going to get cut in two. You'll stay right there in that stick until somebody comes and gets you out. Your [safety] belt will cut you in two. I saw that happen once and helped take the man down. Never want to see any more of it. It will break him backward that way and he's hanging there doubled over, backward. Just imagine what agony he was in there for a moment."[24] Some high-lead loggers fell to their deaths when they accidentally cut their safety ropes with their axes. Some were blown off the tree by a gust of wind, or died from rigging accidents or broken cables.

Despite all the accidents, there was little medical care in the isolated lumber camps. Doctors and hospitals were miles and hours away. "When there was an accident," recalled Stoneburg, "as an ordinary rule, everything in that particular area would cease right then and the men would rush to offer assistance, give assistance if possible . . . as much as possible."[25] If a man survived but was unable to work again because of disability, the boss did not have to compensate him for the injury or the future inability to earn a living. As George Hunsby put it, "If you got hurt, it was just your bad luck."[26] Although there were no laws until 1911 requiring employers to compensate workers for injuries they received on the job, Hunsby's experience was that the employers weren't totally heartless: "As a general rule, the logging camp operator would supply something. He probably would pay the person's hospital expenses, you know, and probably would help the family."[27]

But no matter how many new dangers technology created, the logger's worst enemy was always fire. The amount of wood left in the forest as waste created perfect conditions for forest fires. In 1902 the entire Pacific Northwest suffered a series of deadly fires at the end of an unusually dry summer. Homer McGee was driving a team of horses hauling kindling to camp when he saw a fire racing toward him. "Even the stream seemed to be on fire," reported a friend. "He tried to get the team turned around but had no time to do more than jerk the lines. He jumped headlong into water already hot to the touch and buried himself as deeply as he could under a muddy overhang of roots. He prayed, living a horrible, searing lifetime in the minutes it took the worst of the blast to pass over him. . . . When he dared crawl out over the hot ashes, he saw the charred horses and wagon iron. He groped his way along the edge of the river to the log landing, marked by the twisted piles of steel that had been the donkey engine. Some of the men had escaped. Eight others, including his two brothers, had been burned to shapeless heaps."[28]

Early loggers had little chance of stopping a forest fire.

Given the danger and the unpleasant conditions, who chose to work in the logging camps, and why? The short answer is that logging employment was available; it was not hard to learn; it required strength, not literacy; and the money was not bad most of the time, even after paying for the room and board the company provided.

"The striking thing about the California lumbermen is their diversity," wrote an observer of life in an early redwood camp. "Almost every European nationality is represented—French, German, Norwegian, Spanish, English, Scotch, and Irish, not to speak of Americans, Chinese, and

Indians."[29] This was a time of significant immigration. Native Americans worked both in logging camps and sawmills, but few African-Americans were employed in the woods.

Surveys around the turn of the century showed more than 90 percent of the loggers were bachelors. In the early 1900s foremen did not want to hire married men. Living in isolated areas, without any female companionship, families, or recreational opportunities, made the backcountry camps rowdy and gave rise to the stereotype of the wild, footloose logger who never stayed anyplace very long.

Life in the woods and the mills was, like railroad life, almost entirely a man's world. Few women were in the logging camps until after World War I. There were occasional women cooks, who were married to loggers in the camps, but it was rare. An early-twentieth-century survey of three western states showed only 74 women employed in the logging industry, compared to 20,183 men.

Married or single, the vast majority of loggers were only temporary employees. Some were only temporarily loggers, like the Anderson brothers. George Hunsby worked with them at one camp. "[They] would take turn about," he recalled. "One . . . of 'em would work all year in the logging camp and the other would be developing the farm. And, the next year, they would reverse it. And, after awhile . . . through hard work, they developed the Hillview Dairy. . . . And, there was lots of farmers that split the same way, that spent part of their life out in the logging camp. Because there was no money coming in on the farms. That was all outgo, until they got the farm stocked up and got enough land cleared so that they go in the dairy business or poultry business."[30]

More typical was George Hunsby. He was a logger his entire working life, but was a bachelor who liked to move around. "That's how I happened to work in so many different camps," he said, "because I'd only work a few months in a camp and then I'd have so much money, I wouldn't know what to do with it. So, I'd have to go off somewheres and spend it. Well, then I'd have to go to work again. I never thought anything about saving any money. That was the last thing that entered my mind."[31]

Peter Jaspers, who started working in the camps as a teenager, lived his life the same way. "If I didn't like it, I just quit. I don't know why, but I think I must have been in fifteen different camps on the whole Columbia River here. And if I'd get wet, my back would get real wet and get cold, 'Aw heck with this, I'm going to quit.' Well, the other one was just as bad."[32]

The story of the logging industry would not be complete without including the role played by mill workers. Very few uses exist for 200-foot-long logs. Without mills to turn the trees into pieces suitable for bridges, wharf supports, shingles, doors, building timbers, and hundreds of other specialized uses, there would have been no market for the labor of the lumberjacks.

Although there were comparable numbers of men employed in both industries, little has been written about mill workers. They had no mythic heroes representing them, as the lumberjacks had Paul Bunyan. They lived a more ordinary life, worked more regular hours, lived in town with their wives and children. In 1870 Charles Scammon, a reporter for the *Overland Monthly*, observed: "The change from camp life to that in the mill-towns is quite pleasing to one who has passed months amid the solitudes of the sombre forests. . . ."[33]

This 1907 group shows the ethnic diversity among sawmill laborers.

What they did have in common with lumberjacks was increasing numbers of ways to be injured by the heavy, sharp, steam-driven machinery. The large mills used many kinds of steam-powered machinery, all fueled by burning the sawdust created as a by-product of cutting the logs. A steam engine pulled the logs from the water into the mill; a steam-powered circular saw cut them into planks. A steam-powered edger cut the planks into boards, and a steam-powered trimmer made the edges even. A steam-powered planing machine smoothed the rough edges.

By the 1890s new equipment further increased the mills' output. Changing from circular saws to band saws had reduced the amount of wood wasted in the mills and increased tenfold the amount of lumber that a mill could

A typical boiler room at a sawmill

produce each day. New equipment also created more ways to get hurt.

George Hunsby saw a man go headfirst into an edger. His co-worker's gunnysack apron became tangled on some rollers, which had spiked teeth for pulling the timber into the edger. The machine pulled his head between the main rollers, and his hand between two smaller rollers. When the machine stopped, "it had stripped all his clothes off except his shoes . . . he was stark naked. And there he was wedged in between these two great rolls. . . . We wound backwards to wind him out . . . it had just plucked his ears right out. They were layin' at the foot of the machine, and I picked 'em up and threw 'em out through the window afterwards. . . . He had a big hole gouged in his chest, and the arm that went into these small rolls was broken in several places."[34] The man lived only because the machine stopped almost immediately. While this mishap sounds grisly, it was by no means unusual.

Jun Ishii also witnessed the dangers in millwork. His friend Mr. Moriyasu's job was "to make fuel for the steam engines by throwing odds and ends of lumber into the chopper," Ishii remembered. "But by mistake he fell into the machine and was chopped to pieces. We wanted to have a funeral for him, but there was nothing left of his body. We hunted through the chopped-up wood until we found a piece of flesh about as big as a fifty-cent-piece, and went ahead with the funeral."[35]

Sawmill fires were also a significant danger. Every board sawed created sawdust, which burns very easily. Although the steam machinery in the mills burned sawdust and waste pieces for fuel, only half was used up this way. If a fire started accidentally, it would roar out of control easily in the sawdust shavings. Charles Scammon reported: "In order to get rid of the surplus dust, edgings, and the general debris, it is found necessary to burn them. . . . A tramway is usually run out a short distance, to obviate any danger to the building by fire, and the whole mass of combustible matter . . . is thrown into a heap and burned to ashes. Strange as it may seem, these fires, once kindled, have been kept constantly going for years. At night one sees the smoldering blaze, and by day the stifling smoke rolls upward, or drifts and settles along the wooded shores."[36] Like the smoke that was always present, it seemed as if the forests and logging would continue forever.

6

WHAT DIFFERENCE DID THEY MAKE?

In 1840 the face of the western half of what is now the United States looked very different. Virgin forests covered much of the Pacific Coast and the mountain regions. The population was very small—perhaps a total of 25,000 people on the whole Pacific coastline, and fewer in the interior. The western United States was known and used only by Native American peoples, trappers, and pioneers willing to make a lengthy journey and create a home under primitive conditions. The few western migrants and travelers came by several routes. Some traveled from the East Coast around South America 17,000 miles by ship; this voyage required at least 100 days continuously at sea. Some who sailed from the East Coast left the Atlantic Ocean at the Isthmus of Panama, boarded a riverboat as far as it could go, and continued to Panama City on the Pacific Coast by horse, wagon, or coach. Then, if they had not died of tropical diseases or cholera crossing Panama, they sailed north to San Francisco. The third option was traveling by wagon west from Missouri to California or Oregon through unsettled wilderness, with no communities to provide supplies or shelter along the way.

What difference did the railroaders make?

Thirty years later a transcontinental railroad connected the Pacific region to the rest of the country. In another thirty years, in 1900, hundreds of thousands of miles of track connected most of the country. Americans could afford to ship heavy, bulky commodities—ores, crops, lumber—from inland or mountainous areas where they were produced to where there was a market for them. They could reach and harvest remote resources, such as timber, that were not at the tidewater or along rivers.

The railroads also encouraged settlement of much of the West. Sales of millions of acres of land belonging to the railroads had populated the rural regions. Most of them,

An 1898 town in Washington that was built along the Great Northern Railway

except the Great Northern Railroad, had received help in paying their construction costs from the federal government in the form of land grants. Congress gave land on either side of the railway route to the railroads and allowed them to sell it to help finance their track construction.

The railroads had another reason for wanting to sell the land along the rails. If it was settled, and crops were grown, if sawmills sawed lumber to be sold, and towns and factories were built, people would use the railroads to ship their products to distant markets. So the railroads advertised and recruited widely in Europe, seeking immigrants to come and settle in the areas where they owned federal land.

What difference did logging make?

The development of America, and the construction of all its industries, required uncounted billions of board feet of lumber. Every mile of railroad track required 2,600 large wooden ties. Mines needed timber to support the walls and tunnels. Western America's homes, factories, farms, businesses, and public buildings were largely built of board lumber. Sometimes those buildings had to be rebuilt several times. San Francisco, for example, burned to the ground six times between December 1849 and June 1851, and was rebuilt with lumber each time. Since the forests of Maine and the enormous white pine forests of the upper Midwest had been exhausted by 1900, western logging provided the needed material. Without the loggers, America would look very different today.

Those loggers would hardly recognize their replacements and descendants three generations later. The tools and skills needed to do the job in 1920 were far different from those in 1850. Bull-team logging gave way to high-

The great San Francisco fire of 1851

lead logging using steam engines. Small family operations and small camps were replaced by 1,000-man crews in improved working and living conditions. Only two things stayed the same—the hard physical labor and the danger. In 1920 the Washington State Safety Board described the timber industry as "more deadly than war,"[1] because more men had died doing lumber industry jobs in 1920 than had been killed in the Spanish-American War of 1898.

"Nobody then thought the timber would ever run out. You could stand on the top of the highest hill you could find, and see nothing but timber to the west, the southwest, and the northwest,"[2] wrote Joseph Pierre, who was born in

1906 in backwoods timber country. His family thought of themselves as pioneers. "I, the eighth and last child of a western pioneer family, was born . . ."[3] he wrote, in a log cabin, in timber country that was vast, wild, and untouched by roads. His family homesteaded and worked in the logging industry in the old-growth forests in south-western Washington State after the invention of the donkey engine and the logging railroad. They were pioneering as late as 1906 because there was still virgin timber. Once the trees were gone, the pioneer days were over.

SOURCE NOTES

1. WESTERN LOGGING FROM SETTLEMENT TO STEAM

1. Linda Allen, *Washington Songs and Lore* (Spokane, Wash.: Melior Publications, 1988), 16.

2. *Memorial and Biographical History of Northern California* (Chicago: Lewis Publishing Co., 1891).

3. Ibid.

4. Louise Clappe (Dame Shirley), *The Shirley Letters: From the California Mines, 1851–1852*. Edited by Carl I. Wheat. (New York: Knopf, 1961), 86.

5. Fred Lockley, *Conversations with Pioneer Women* (Eugene, Ore.: Rainy Day Press, 1981), 286.

6. Arthur Armstrong Denny, *Pioneer Days on Puget Sound* (Seattle: C. B. Bagley, 1888), 13, 35.

7. Robert A. Bennett, *A Small World of Our Own: Authentic Pioneer Stories of the Pacific Northwest from the Old Settlers Contest of 1892* (Walla Walla, Wash.: Pioneer Press, 1985), 83.

8. Denny, *Pioneer Days on Puget Sound*, 37.

9. Caroline C. Leighton, *Life at Puget Sound with Sketches of Travel in Washington Territory, British Columbia, Oregon, and California 1865–1881* (Boston: Lee and Shepard, 1884), 26.

10. Ibid.

11. Bennett, *A Small World of Our Own*, 48.

12. Ibid.

13. Atlanta Georgia Long Thompson, *The Daughter of a Pioneer: A True Story of Life in Early Colorado* (Portland, Ore.: Binford and Mort, 1982), 33.

14. Ibid., 33–34.

15. Ibid., 34.

16. Ibid.

17. Washington State Oral/Aural History Program (WSO/AP), Oral History (Microform), Washington State Oral/Aural History Program (Olympia, Wash.: State Archives, 1977), transcript of George Hunsby interview, 7, tape 1.

18. WSO/AP, transcript of Ted Swanson interview, 20, tape 1.

2. BUILDING THE FIRST TRANSCONTINENTAL RAILROAD

1. Charles M. Gates, *Readings in Pacific Northwest History: Washington, 1790–1895* (Seattle: University Bookstore, 1941), 197.

2. Samuel Bowles, *Across the Continent: A Summer's Journey to the Rocky Mountains, the Mormons, and Pacific States, with Speaker Colfax* (Springfield, Mass.: S. Bowles, 1865).

3. Lynne Rhodes Mayer and Kenneth E. Vose, eds., *Makin' Tracks: The Story of the Transcontinental Railroad in the Pictures and Words of the Men Who Were There* (New York: Praeger, 1975), 86.

4. Ibid.

5. Ibid., 97.

6. John H. Williams, *A Great and Shining Road* (New York: Times Books, 1988), 151.

7. Mayer and Vose, *Makin' Tracks*, 97.

8. Ibid., 76.

9. Ibid., 78.

10. Ibid., 79.

11. Ibid., 74.

12. Ibid., 74–75.

13. Ibid., 102.

14. Ibid.

15. Ibid., 25.

16. Ibid., 28.

17. Ibid.

18. Ibid., 40–41.

19. Ibid., 44.

3. THE RAILROADS EXPAND

1. Gates, *Readings in Pacific Northwest History*, 204.

2. Harry N. Majors, ed., "A Railroad Survey of the Sauk and Wenatchee Rivers in 1870, D. C. Linsley," *Northwest Discovery*, vol. 2, no. 4 (April 1981): 208.

3. John Frank Stevens, *An Engineer's Recollections* (New York: McGraw-Hill, 1936), 24.

4. Ibid., 24–25.

5. Joseph A. Noble, *From Cab to Caboose: Fifty Years of Railroading* (Norman, Okla.: University Press, 1964), 11–12.

6. Donald G. Harvey, "Uncle Charlie Was a Railroader," in *The Pacific Northwesterner*, vol. 22, no. 4 (Fall 1978): 62.

7. Ibid.

8. Ibid.

9. Kazuo Ito, *Issei: A History of Japanese Immigrants in North America* (Seattle: Executive Committee for Publication of Issei, 1973), 300.

10. Ibid., 304–305.

11. Montana Historical Society Staff, eds., *Not in Precious Metals Alone: A Manuscript History of Montana* (Helena, Mont.: The Society, 1976), 128.

12. Ibid.

4. WORKING FOR THE RAILROAD

1. Walter Licht, *Working for the Railroad: The Organization of Work in the Nineteenth Century* (Princeton, New Jersey: Princeton University Press, 1983), 183.

2. Dee Brown, *Hear That Lonesome Whistle Blow* (New York: Holt, Rinehart and Winston, 1977), 175.

3. Ibid., 174.

4. Chauncey Del French, *Railroadman* (New York: Macmillan, 1938), 118.

5. Ibid.

6. Noble, *From Cab to Caboose*, 61.

7. Harvey, *Uncle Charlie Was a Railroader*, 61.

8. Brown, *Hear That Lonesome Whistle Blow*, 178.

9. Ito, *Issei*, 296.

10. Ibid., 309.

11. Ibid.

12. Ibid., 297.

13. Ibid., 313.

14. Ibid., 303.

5. LOGGING AFTER 1880

1. Thompson, *Daughter of a Pioneer*, 34.

2. WSO/AP, transcript of interview with William Bighill, 5.

3. WSO/AP, transcript of interview with Frank McKinnon, 10.

4. Ron Strickland, *River Pigs and Cayuses: Oral Histories from the Pacific Northwest* (San Francisco: Lexikos, 1984), 88–89.

5. Ibid., 91.

6. WSO/AP, transcript of interview with Frank Kordes, 19.

7. Strickland, *River Pigs and Cayuses*, 87.

8. Ibid.

9. WSO/AP, McKinnon, 13.

10. Strickland, *River Pigs and Cayuses*, 87.

11. Ibid.

12. WSO/AP, transcript of interview with Peter Jaspers, 4.

13. WSO/AP, Kordes, 9.

14. Allen, *Washington Songs and Lore*, 24.

15. WSO/AP, transcript of interview with George Hunsby, 10, tape 1.

16. WSO/AP, transcript of interview with Joseph Stoneburg, 28.

17. Sam Churchill, *Don't Call Me Ma* (Garden City, New York: Doubleday, 1977), 37.

18. WSO/AP, Jaspers.

19. WSO/AP, Hunsby, 9.

20. WSO/AP, Jaspers, 3–4.

21. WSO/AP, Bighill, 8.

22. WSO/AP, Stoneburg, 7

23. WSO/AP, Bighill, 10.

24. WSO/AP, Stoneburg, 7.

25. Ibid., 28.

26. WSO/AP, Hunsby, 3, tape 2.

27. Ibid.

28. Editors of Time-Life Books, with text by Richard L. Williams, *The Old West: The Loggers* (New York: Time-Life Books, 1976), 158.

29. Ibid., 133.

30. WSO/AP, Hunsby, 3, tape 2.

31. Ibid.

32. WSO/AP, Jaspers, 5.

33. Charles Scammon, "Lumbering in Washington Territory," in *Overland Monthly* 5 (July 1870): 58.

34. WSO/AP, Hunsby 5, tape 2.

35. Ito, *Issei*, 410.

36. Scammon, "Lumbering in Washington Terrritory," 59.

6. WHAT DIFFERENCE DID THEY MAKE?

1. Andrew Prouty, *More Deadly Than War!: Pacific Coast Logging, 1827–1981* (New York: Garland, 1985).

2. Joseph H. Pierre, *When Timber Stood Tall* (Seattle: Superior Publishing Co., 1979), 29.

3. Ibid., 25.

FURTHER READING

BOOKS

Aaseng, Nathan. *From Rags to Riches.* Minneapolis: Lerner, 1990.

Alter, Judith. *Growing Up in the Old West.* Chicago: Watts, 1991.

———. *Women of the Old West.* New York: Watts, 1989.

Bakeless, John, ed. *The Journals of Lewis and Clark.* New York: Penguin, 1964.

Bennett, Robert Allen. *We'll All Go Home in the Spring.* Walla Walla, Wash.: Pioneer Press, 1984.

Binns, Archie. *Peter Skene Ogden: Fur Trader.* Portland, Ore.: Binford and Mort, 1967.

Blumberg, Rhoda. *The Great American Gold Rush.* New York: Macmillan, 1989.

Brown, Dee. *Gentle Tamers: Women in the Old Wild West.* Lincoln: University of Nebraska Press, 1968.

———. *Hear That Lonesome Whistle Blow: Railroads in the West.* New York: Holt, 1977.

Carter, Harvey L. *Dear Old Kit.* Norman: University of Oklahoma Press, 1968.

Clappe, Louise (Dame Shirley). *The Shirley Letters: From the California Mines, 1850–1852*. Edited by Carl I. Wheat. New York: Knopf, 1961.

Clemens, Samuel Langhorne. *Roughing It*. New York: Holt, Rinehart and Winston, 1965.

De Nevi, Don, and Noel Moholy. *Junípero Serra*. New York: Harper and Row, 1985.

Erickson, Paul. *Daily Life in a Covered Wagon*. Washington, D.C.: Preservation Press, 1994.

Fischer, Christiane, ed. *Let Them Speak for Themselves: Women in the American West, 1849–1900*. Hamden, Conn.: Archon, 1977.

Fisher, Leonard Everett. *The Oregon Trail*. New York: Holiday, 1990.

Harte, Bret. *The Luck of Roaring Camp*. Providence, Rhode Island: Jamestown, 1976.

Hoobler, Dorothy, and Thomas Hoobler. *Treasure in the Stream: The Story of a Gold Rush Girl*. Morristown, New Jersey: Silver Burdett, 1991.

Jessett, Thomas E. *Chief Spokan Garry*. Minneapolis: T. S. Denison, 1960.

Johnson, Paul C., ed. *The California Missions*. Menlo Park, Cal.: Lane Book, 1964.

Katz, William. *The Black West*. Seattle: Open Hand, 1987.

Lapp, Rudolph. *Blacks in Gold Rush California*. New Haven: Yale University Press, 1977.

Lasky, Kathryn. *Beyond the Divide*. New York: Dell, 1986.

Levy, Jo Ann. *They Saw the Elephant*. Hamden, Conn.: Archon, 1990.

Lewis, Oscar. *Sutter's Fort: Gateway to the Gold Fields*. New York: Knopf, 1976.

Luchetti, Cathy, and Carol Olwell. *Women of the West*. Berkeley: Antelope Island Press, 1982.

McNeer, May. *The California Gold Rush*. New York: Random House, 1987.

Meltzer, Milton. *The Chinese Americans: A History in Their Own Words.* New York: HarperCollins, 1980.

Morris, Juddi. *The Harvey Girls: The Women Who Civilized the West.* New York: Walker, 1994.

Moynihan, Ruth B., Susan Armitage, and Christiane Fischer Duchamp, eds. *So Much to Be Done: Women Settlers on the Mining and Ranching Frontier.* Lincoln: University of Nebraska Press, 1990.

Nabakov, Peter. *Native American Testimony: An Anthology of Indian and White Relations, First Encounter to Dispossession.* New York: HarperCollins, 1972.

Rappaport, Doreen, ed. *American Women: Their Lives in Their Words.* New York: HarperCollins, 1992.

Ray, Delia. *Gold, the Klondike Adventure.* New York: Lodestar, 1989.

Schlissel, Lillian. *Women's Diaries of the Westward Journey.* New York: Shocken, 1982.

Smith, Carter. *Bridging the Continent: A Sourcebook on the American West.* Brookfield, Conn.: Millbrook Press, 1992.

Steber, Rick. *Grandpa's Stories.* Prineville, Ore.: Bonanza, 1991.

Stewart, George R. *The Pioneers Go West.* New York: Random House, 1987.

Stratton, Joanna. *Pioneer Women.* New York: Simon and Schuster, 1982.

The Trailblazers. *The Old West.* New York: Time-Life Books, 1979.

Tunis, Edwin. *Frontier Living.* New York: HarperCollins, 1976.

Van Steenwyk, Elizabeth. *The California Gold Rush: West with the Forty-niners.* Chicago: Watts, 1991.

Watt, James W. *Journal of Mule Train Packing in Eastern Washington in the 1860s.* Fairfield, Wash.: Ye Galleon Press, 1978.

Weis, Norman D. *Helldorados, Ghosts and Camps of the Old Southwest.* Caldwell, Idaho: Caxton Printers, 1977.

Wilder, Laura Ingalls. *West from Home.* New York: HarperCollins, 1974.

Wilson, Elinor. *Jim Beckwourth: Black Mountain Man and War Chief of the Crows.* Norman: University of Oklahoma Press, 1972.

Young, Alida O. *Land of the Iron Dragon.* New York: Doubleday, 1978.

TAPES AND COMPUTER SOFTWARE

American West: Myth and Reality, Clear View, CD-ROM.

Dare, Bluff, or Die, Software Tool Works, CD-ROM, DOS.

Miner's Cave, MECC, Apple II.

Morrow, Honere. *On to Oregon!* Recorded Books, Inc., Prince Frederick, Md. Three cassettes.

Murphy's Minerals, MECC, Apple II.

Oregon Trail II, CD-ROM, Windows.

The Oregon Trail, MECC, Apple II, MS-DOS, 1990.

Santa Fe Trail (Educational Activities).

Steber, Rick. *Grandpa's Stories.* Bonanza. Cassette.

Wagons West, Focus Media, 485 South Broadway, Suite 12, Hicksville, New York, 11801.

INDEX

Irish immigrant workers, 31,
35, 53, 74

Japanese immigrant workers,
44, 54, 55, 56, 57
Jaspers, Peter, 64, 69, 76

Kordes, Frank, 62, 64, 65

Leighton, Caroline, 19, 20
log schooners, 18, 20
loggers
    clothing worn by, 67, 68
    diet of, 62
    hardships endured by, 18,
        22, 24, 58, 62, 64, 68, 69,
        83
    hazards endured by, 15, 16,
        22, 23, 61, 62, 64, 72, 73,
        74, 77, 78, 83
    living conditions among, 62,
        64, 65, 66, 67, 72, 74
    wages for, 59, 60, 69, 74, 76
logging jobs
    buckers, 23
    bullwhackers, 24, 59
    chokermen, 60
    firemen, 59
    high riggers, 70, 72
    logging camp cooks, 62, 63,
        64, 75
    punchers, 60
    river pigs, 60, 61, 62
    splitters, 59
    whistle punks, 50
Long, Attie, 21, 22, 58
lumber, 14, 15, 17, 18, 19, 20,
    77, 82

Marshall, John, 15
McGee, Homer, 73
McKinnon, Frank, 60, 63
mill workers, 76, 77, 78, 79
mining, 17, 34
Missouri, 27
Missouri River, 28, 29
Montana Central Railroad, 45
Murphy, John, 39, 40

Native Americans, 11, 14, 75, 80
Northern Pacific Railroad, 40,
    42, 45, 69

Oregon Territory, 14, 16, 18, 20,
    25, 80
oxen, 21, 22, 23, 24, 26, 58, 59

Pacific Coast, 13, 19, 80
Panama Canal, 52
Pierre, Joseph, 83, 84
Pope & Talbot Company, 20
Pope, Army General John, 29
Prescott, Charlie, 42, 43, 44, 51,
    52
Puget Sound, 18

railroad workers
    clothing worn by, 55
    diet of 56, 57
    hardships endured by, 27,
        28, 40, 41, 42, 55, 56
    hazards endured by, 29, 30,
        33, 34, 36, 37, 38, 46, 47,
        48, 49, 50
    living conditions for, 31, 32,
        42, 44, 55, 56, 57
    wages for, 43, 51, 55